Mad John's Walk

Five Leaves Bookshop Occasional Papers

The Current Status of Jerusalem by Edward Said
978-1-910170-09-0, 32 pages, £4

Doctor Who and the Communist: Malcolm Hulke and his career in television by Michael Herbert
978-1-910170-08-3, 32 pages, £4

Strengthening Democracy in Post-conflict Northern Ireland by Maria Power
978-1-910170-16-8, 32 pages, £4

Anarchy 38: Nottingham by Freedom Press
978-1-910170-18-2, 32 pages, £4

How We Live and How We Might Live by William Morris
978-1-910170-26-7, 28 pages, £4

Harper Lee and the American South by Katie Hamilton
978-1-910170-27-4, 28 pages, £4

That Precious Strand of Jewishness that Challenges Authority by Leon Rosselson
978-1-910170-33-5, 28 pages, £4

Mad John's Walk by John Gallas
978-1-910170-41-0, 16 pages, £3

Available from Five Leaves or from other bookshops worldwide.
All prices include UK postage if ordered direct from
Five Leaves Bookshop.

www.fiveleavesbookshop.co.uk

Mad John's Walk
with John Clare from High Beach
Asylum to Northborough

John Gallas

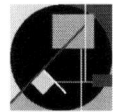

Five Leaves Bookshop Occasional Papers

Mad John's Walk
by John Gallas

Published in 2017 by Five Leaves Bookshop
14a Long Row, Nottingham NG1 2DH
www.fiveleavesbookshop.co.uk

Five Leaves Bookshop Occasional Paper 8
ISBN: 978-1-910170-41-0

Copyright © John Gallas, 2017

Designed and typeset by Five Leaves Bookshop

Printed by Russell Press in Nottingham, UK

Against the Biography of John Clare

How dull and vexing is it, that each man
though free to plough, still turns the self-same ditch.
I looked for more. At Helpstone yesterday,
I threw myself into a stubbled field
with half an apple and the Book of Clare
to read a store of verslings midst the bees,
the timid mouse, the brook, the flibbling trees,
the hedgehog and the lark, the nimbling hare
and all the bosky fronds and friends revealed
by half a sun in wigs of clouds. The hay
stood stacked in stooks, and down the half-flowered twitch
the planted pylons strod. So I began.
Begin in gladness.
Pass to madness.
End in sadness.

Did I expect some *other* life, to lead
my troubled share about another earth?
Some stumbling revolution of our time?
It rained: I stayed. The rawky pages blopped
with disappointed summer, and the wind
disturbed to little frenzies all the tops
of witchen, whin and woodbine, and the copse,
with dark green mouth agapen, ducked and dinned
upon its cracking brig. Enough. I dropped
my core into a thurrow. Word and rhyme,
leaf and line have had their pennyworth,
and common died amongst the common weed.
Begin in gladness.
Pass to madness.
End in sadness.

Mad John's Walk

175 years ago, John Clare, residing at Matthew Allen's High Beach Private Asylum in Epping Forest, decided to go home. 'Felt very melancholy,' he wrote, two days before. 'Fell in with some gypsies, one of whom offered to assist in my escape from the madhouse.' Two days later, he was off.

His route, via the Great North Road, was around eighty miles. I thought this doable. First, I Googled walking directions from each place he had remembered to the next. Then, I bought a pair of Skechers, with Memory Foam Feet. I took a spare T-shirt, a spare pair of socks, a rollable raincoat, a hat, the Penguin *Clare*, a notebook and pen, and my iPod Fitness App, to measure each damned step along the way. John C. had old boots, and nothing else. I also had a bank account.

His own account is unfailingly practical: the state of his feet, and his boots, the direction he was going, the people he met, and the search for food and a place to sleep were his only concerns. There is little creative in a desperate pedestrian. And so it proved. The place of his homes, Helpston and Northborough, I know and love. If madness was missing, I felt still that I held his hand all the way, but that we did not talk about Life. Sometimes, that is Poetry.

Day 1: 48,477 steps, 7 hours & 20 minutes, 26.88 miles. High Beach Asylum to the Baker Arms at Bayford.

The wall of Matthew Allen's Asylum, now a private home, has a blue plaque: *John Clare the Famous Poet lived here 1837–1841*. It was exactly 12.00, and my first Clare-town was Enfield. He missed his way early, and so did I: ...*til I passed the Labour-in-vain public house, where a person who came out of the door told me the way* (JC); til I asked three youths wheeling a great black pram with silver fittings, ponderous as a coffin, down South Ordnance Road (JG). There were several Enfields: a Chase, a Town, a Highway, an Island Village, a Lock and a Wash. I asked for the Town. In half an hour I was in Silver Street, putting three pages of directions in my bag, and taking out the next.

To Stevenage. My Google map informed me this would take seven hours and twenty-nine minutes. It was already three o'clock. For JC, this part of the journey was either too easy, or not worthy of memory: *Steering ahead, meeting no enemy and fearing none, I reached Stevenage*, via the Great York Road. This torrent of cars, unending and unfriendly, is denied the walker now. The famous, straight road that JC knew would take him nearly home, once leafy and deserted, was now a roaring speedway. I am sure the absence of memory along these twenty miles was prompted by the absence of his greatest care: that he was going the wrong way. He was set for all. I was lost within a mile.

I stopped at a Turkish garage, where four large men in white shirts held their smartphones at various angles, and directed me back to the Civic Centre in Silver Street. I began again, and soon passed through a mileage of Garden Centres, padding like a Hobbit in the land of Men, past giant fibreglass strawberries with cafés inside, towering kangaroos, bunnies and immense, high fences draped with rampant climbers, enormously vigorous. I then passed a house called Claregate.

The sky was darkling. I asked three women, orange in the sunset, if there was anywhere nearby to stay. They told me there was somewhere that would 'make yer eyes water'; but that down Carbone Hill, and through Newgate Street, there was, also, on the right, the Baker Arms, at Bayford, which did rooms.

Two children behind the bar gave me my keys. The room was vast, and had a bath. I stood at the sash window, which I threw wide open, and looked into the quiet darkness of the village street. Unfortunately, I had forgotten to find its name. I think I was in Hertfordshire.

Day 2: 66,706 steps, 9 hours & 44 minutes, 34.80 miles.
The Baker Arms to the Rose & Crown at Baldock.

I strode out early. But quite the wrong way. The street that passed in front of my window was Ashdene Road, which I began the day by searching for two miles away. The frustration and anger visited on a pedestrian by going out of his way is crushing; with John C., it was an obsession. At Stevenage (his first night) he wrote: *I lay down with my head towards the north, to show myself the steering point in the morning.*

But Nature is a balm. The bright, sunny morning, leading me by dug stubble-fields and whispering greeneries, through Broad Green to St Mary's Lane, quickly restored me to everything. At a farm gate, in a spot of dappled lightness, I decided to open, in the random manner of a bibliomantic, my Penguin *Clare*.

I see the sky
Smile on the meanest spot
Giving to all that creep or walk or flye
A calm and cordial lot

At Hertford, I picked an acorn from a tree, and put it in my pack. At Datchworth I drank two bottles of Evian water. At Stevenage, I hurried through. Leaving the town, on a hot, wide pavement, I saw a small orange lying in my way. I looked at it. What, I asked myself, would John Clare do? Naturally, I ate it.

At Back Lane high trees turned the way into a narrow and wet darkness redolent of dew and liquid foliage. Google told me I was about to enter Damask Green Road. I thought it would be laced with emerald lawns and bushes, breathing a green intoxication from fields made of bolts of cloth laid on the land. Then I got lost. Damask Green Road remains a fair thought sewn upon a landscape. In fact, it contained the Cricketers Arms, where I asked the way to Clothall Road.

Here, two people involved with a concrete-mixer told me that only Baldock could possibly accommodate me. I hurried down the main road into town, facing the terrible onslaught of rush hour. I leapt from tussock to weed along the roadside as cars driven with furious intent lifted my bag off my back each second in their slipstream. I longed for 1841.

It was Baldock Rock weekend. I took a room at the Rose & Crown; small, shabby, and directly above the main door, the street, and the Rock room. 'I hope,' said the landlady, 'you're not thinking of getting any sleep.' But even the Heavy Metal Holiday below could not keep me awake.

Day 3: 60,664 steps, 8 hours & 52 minutes, 32.06 miles. The Rose & Crown at Baldock to St. Neots.

I left my lodging by the way I got in, and thanked God for His kindness in procuring it. For anything in a famine is better than nothing, and any place that giveth the weary rest is a blessing.

After two mis-starts, I was determined to do right this morning. It was drizzling softly. I immediately asked a man with a dog the way to Claybush Road. His directions were perfect. I strod on, while the rain thinned in a glitter of air, along a beautiful, waving road, to Ashwell. Here, a child asked me, 'Why are you walking?' If he had had a shilling, John Clare would surely have ridden: to do this journey free of care seemed to me there, in shady Gardiners Lane, to do it for John C., this time without pain. Soon, however, I told myself, I would eat grass, as he did, just to see.

At the junction of Cambridge Road, I was seized by the fancy that I was being followed by a very tall and thin cow. I hardly dared turn around. I knew there was no real cow behind me, but I could hear the vision, which was alarming. As I continued not to look, its features fell into more and more detail; flat, small ears, an elongated snout, large, mournful, green eyes, sunken shoulders, and legs long as stilts. Whatever it was, it was not The Muse.

I reached Sutton, where churchfolk with armfuls of flowers, directed me onto a public footpath through Pegnut Woods. It was wet and beautiful, with little bridges over twiddling streams, grass steaming in the sun, and jewelled insects zooming strangely high in the trees.

In Potton, John C. called at a house to ask for a light for his pipe. I sat on a bench and ate an apple, and drank a quantity of chocolate milk.

After another brief shower of rain, I went on. By now, John C's legs were 'knocked up', and he was ...*hopping with a crippled foot; for the gravel had got into [his] old shoes, one of which had now nearly lost the sole*. I bounced out of town in my Skechers.

From Potton to St Neots, I had printed my directions backwards. The resulting confusion was beyond all bloody proportion. I asked directions from every person I came across. At Cinques Road I went two miles down a hill to find a signpost that said Potton was very near. I trudged back up: I had walked unseeing past a large fingerpost that said 'St Neots 4'.

It was something of a slog. After passing the only thing of interest, a large plantation of elder trees that moaned like widows at a graveside, I entered the annoying suburb of Eynsford, which was very long, in more light drizzle. And then St Neots, where, at the Nags Head, I found a room. Here, John C. sat down to rest on a flint heap, where he was told by 'a gypsy girl' to put something in his hat to keep the crown up, or he would be noticed.

Back in my room at the Nags Head, and quite unnoticed, I took another pop at bibliomancy, with my Penguin.

Youth has no fear of ill by no cloudy days annoyed
But the old man's all hath fled and his hopes have met their doom

I slept the sleep of the Just.

Day 4: 62,875 steps, 9 hours & 20 minutes, 32.85 miles. St Neots to Stilton.

I strod on towards the Great North Road, as directed by Google, where, a mile later, deafened by engines, I was forced to take a footpath alternative to its certain death. It was Google's only mistake. This turned into a very Heaven, all the way to Buckden. Late poppies and birdsong wibbled on all sides. The trees, brighter than bright in the sun, gleamed along the edges of amber fields, like living, silver creatures lined up to watch the tractors putter back and forth, ploughing and turning the earth to chocolate. Here, I thought, of all places, I must pause.

I determined to do two things in this little Paradise: to eat grass, and to find a line in my Penguin that made me weep. To John C., grass tasted 'something like bread', and did him good. I had no need of goodness, and it tasted to me like a pale inkling of beanpod. Standing in the sun, I then wept over

> *That happy sky with here and there*
> *A little cloud that would express*
> *By the slow motions that they wear*
> *They live with peace and quietness*
> *I think so as I see them glide*
> *Thoughts earthly tumults can't destroy*
> *So calm, so soft, so smooth, they ride*
> *I'm sure their errands must be joy*

Buckden was rather grand, but very noisy. The A1 thundered by, a never-ending river of appal. From here, John C. went 'a length of road', and so did I, via Huntingdon Station, and the Stukeleys. I stopped at a garage and ate three jam doughnuts. I then entered the mystery that is Ermine Street.

This was the old Great York Road, and ran along parallel, and very near to the A1. To walk on it was to be in constant fear of being mown down, though it was quite empty. The rushing of cars and trucks so close, so continuous, made me turn and look behind a hundred times, where there was nothing. The way was hung with apple-trees and blackberry bushes that would have delighted John C., who had, by here, resorted to ...*chewing tobacco all day, and eat it when I had done.* It was his lowest point, and his feet were bleeding. I ate like Adam.

I came to the Stilton Cheese, and stayed. Hereabouts, John C. laid down on a gravel causeway, and thought he was a goner. When he rose, and took a direction to Peterborough, he was filled with purpose.

Which would be me, tomorrow.

Day 5: 38,766 steps, 6 hours & 49 minutes, 18.87 miles. Stilton to Northborough, and John Clare's cottage.

I strod on down the A15 in hopeful style, imagining, stupidly, that the path would penetrate the suburbs and deliver me to the city centre. It did not. I retreated to the cycle and pedestrian network that makes of parts of Peterborough a strange and stranded quietness, where businesses are silently busy amongst trees, and bike-riders swish back and forth alone.

Suddenly, I started to limp.

At the city centre, I sat on a bench next to a man with a Pomeranian on a string. The dog stared at me doggedly. I hurried down Lincoln Road, and continued to Walton, where the blister on my right little toe burst in a moment of tiny pain. I passed Walton, and headed for Werrington. Here, while making for The Beehive, John C. was accosted by a woman he thought forward, drunk or mad, who had leapt out of a passing cart. It was his second wife, Patty.

I got in, and was soon at Northborough.

I passed through a deserted park, and came to Werrington. I did not take the bus. And I was glad, for the last 3.6 miles (Google, 1hr 10min) were an English delight. The cycle path to Peakirk was dappled with sunshine through woffling leaves. The lime-green trees, shoulder to shoulder along the way, flickered light at me with delicious calm. I began to feel proud. I entered Foxcovert Lane, which featured a mighty iron railway-crossing bridge, atop which I stood for a few minutes, and looked out over the fields and rooftops that a twenty-first century John C. would have called home. Glinton spire, so beloved of him, rose occasionally at my left.

Peakirk was as quiet as a Monday church, and lit with honey sunlight. I went on, over a little bridge, and glimpsed a spire ahead: Northborough at last. I stopped for a last random Penguin.

The heavens are wrath – the thunder's rattling peal
Rolls like a vast volcano in the sky
Yet nothing starts the apathy I feel
Nor chills with fear eternal destiny

The church spire turned out to be Deeping St James Priory, and straight ahead. I took my left turn, and entered Northborough to the sound of lawnmowers. I opened the gate at John Clare's cottage, and went to touch the front wall. A woman came out, and invited me in for tea. I sat in John Clare's chimney-nook, and had my photo taken. Then I hobbled down Church Street, past the graves of his children, and sat in the garden of The Pack Horse, drinking Guinness, and waiting for my lift.

Upon their great returns, great travellers find change and sadness, hand in hand with discontent, and the paler versions of their expectations.

So here I am hopeless at home – John Clare, July 1841.

We walk on dreams, and into reality.

Total by the App: 145 miles.

*

Mad John's Walk poems

Day 1

Gibbet Hill

The bones hung here for years they say,
Amidst the murderings of crows,
To show how Man disposes those
That take another life away.

The road is still, the fields are hot.
I try my patience to be good;
But ah, the crow flies in my blood,
And consequence is soon forgot.

Day 2

The Hare

I lay inside the lane of wheat,
Immured from wandering and care,
And watched the white stalks bleed with heat,
When through them came a golden hare.

It sat beside me, spare and tall,
And wondered at me where I lay,
But found no use in me at all,
And turned and sadly loped away.

Day 3

The Purpose

The wheat stands up, unbowed and new.
The church stands up behind.
I am the less contented kind,
For all that God can do.

It has its purpose and its law,
And God has his Career;
While I am left to wander here
And wonder what I'm for.

Day 4

The Cows

I hear the cows behind the hedge,
Tearing at the race-root sedge.
The hollow earth is booming-dark.
I hurry down to Brampton Park.

The hedges hem on either hand.
And do the cows imagine me
Stamping through the hollow land,
unforeseeable and free?

Day 5

The Clare Graves, St Andrews, Northborough

I walk to church between the trees.
The way is wide and white.
The moon is hid. The thistles freeze.
Ah, let God come tonight.

For I am colder than a star.
The way is white and dead.
And Heaven seems too far, too far,
And no light shines ahead.